geminations

rich follett
constance stadler

NeoPoiesis Press, LLC

2775 Harbor Ave SW, Suite D, Seattle, WA 98126-2138
Inquiries: Info@NeoPoiesisPress.com
NeoPoiesisPress.com

Copyright © 2023 by Rich Follett and Constance Stadler

All rights reserved. No part of this book may be used or reproduced in any manner whatsoever without express written permission from the publisher except in the case of brief quotations embodied in critical articles and reviews.

Rich Follett and Constance Stadler – geminations
ISBN 979-8-9858336-3-8 (pbk)

1. Poetry. I. Follett, Rich II. Stadler, Constance III. geminations

Library of Congress Control Number: 2023944330

First Edition

Cover Design: Dale Winslow

Printed in the United States of America.

To all those who celebrate and strive to contribute to

the ever-evolving legacy of the Word.

Contents

Introduction i

Poe

aperitif (c.s.) 3

tell-tale torsion (r.f.)..5

Sexton

identity crisis (c.s) 9

devolution (r.f.) 10

Neruda

incantation (c.s.) 15

poieplegia (r.f.)..16

Shakespeare

tubular vision (r.f.) 21

wailing wounded (c.s.) 23

Twain

basilisk (r.f.)...29

coronation (c.s.) 31

Carroll

gehenna (r.f.) 35

radical acceptance (c.s.)..36

Thomas

welsh-flecked romance (c.s.) 39

polypodieæ (r.f.) 40

Miller

hyde (r.f.) 45

cart blench (c.s.) 46

Thoreau

a very thoreau haiku (r.f.) 51

cultural exchange (c.s.) 52

Brooks

evangeline (r.f.) 57

the tragedy of the raft of the medusa (c.s.) 59

Orwell

escher's oubliette (r.f.) 63

impolitic (c.s.) 65

Lee

coquette (c.s.) 69

exogenesis (r.f.) 71

Brontë

scream (c.s.) 75

what singing really is (r.f.) 78

Dickens

fezziwig regards his missus (r.f.) 83

urchin (c.s.) 85

Steinbeck

parable (c.s.) 89

congruence (r.f.) 92

Swenson

purgatorio (c.s.) 97
gautam (r.f.) 99

Sources 101
Acknowledgments 103
About the Authors 105

Introduction

How does the creative process work? It's a question for the ages, and no one has yet claimed credit for stumbling upon a universal answer.

What has never been in question is the surety of cross-fertilization—how the work of writers inspires other writers. Exposure to innovative artists, whether they be novelists, playwrights, or poets, has long been a catalyst for the creation of new work. Walt Whitman's robust devotion contrasts starkly with Emily Dickinson's introspective personal abstraction; when reading Ernest Hemingway and Virginia Woolf, the reader is exposed to entirely different approaches to conceiving a novel and to radically different world views—without Anton Chekhov, we might not have seen a *Glass Menagerie* from Tennessee Williams.

We have engaged in a project to bring to fruition this arc of engagement via comparison. Without a great deal of forethought, we discussed excerpts from the work and the observations of influential writers in an organic poet-to-poet dialogue about the hallmarks of excellence in poetry and prose. Seeking to better understand this animus, we assigned each other a different quote from each author and then responded through poetry. One parameter was absolute: once we gave each other the prompts, no work was shared or discussed until completion. Sources ranged from well-known publications to noteworthy asides, as we jointly believe that both the mind and life of every great artist are works of art in themselves.

This collection features our mutual poetic response to the quotations which we assigned to each other. The results are perhaps as surprising to us as they may be to you, our reader: at times, there was thematic consonance; at other times, the results veered in different directions.

This is the second book we have written together. The first, *Responsorials*, also dealt with paired responses, from the perspective of the male-female dynamic. We found that, in addition to being unique as individuals and artists, our perceptions and interpretations were influenced by gender in surprising and revealing ways. Continuing this ongoing poetic dialogue not only helps us to achieve better understanding of who we are as human beings and as creative artists, but also helps us to appreciate the significance of taking part in an exchange that is as relevant today as it was in the eras of Sappho and Li Bai. We hope that our readers will see our work as an invitation to take part in this timeless and universal colloquy on their own terms, with their own creative partners, and in their own ways.

~ Constance Stadler and Rich Follett

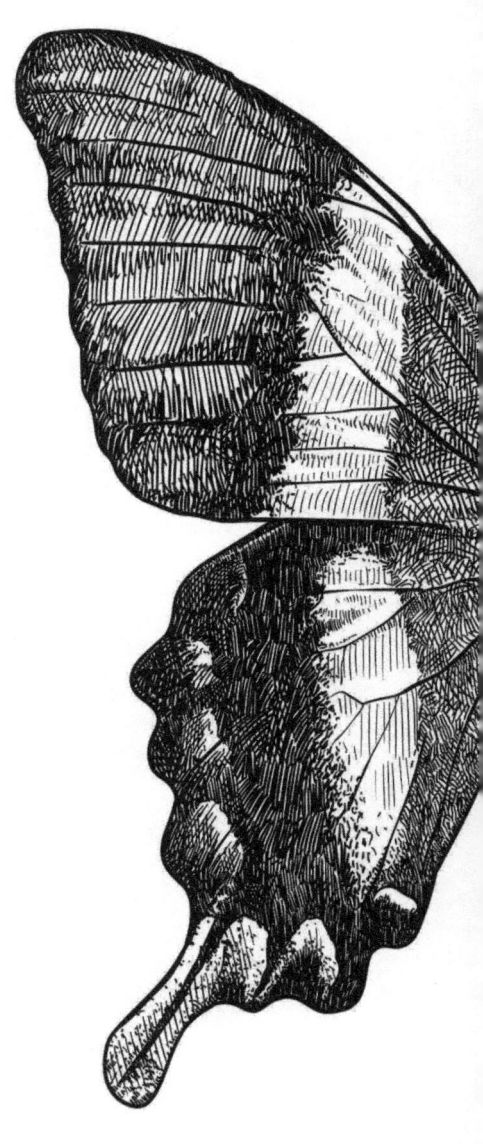

Poe

aperitif (c.s.)

My dear Fortunato, you are luckily met. ~ Edgar Allan Poe

incredulous
offer
      to
             sip
    sovereign elixir
  impelled
               imperium dreams.

  ... the amontillado
the amontillado ...

impregnable provenance
               oloroso majesty

 in whetted anticipation

             reverie arrested:

we shared a concussed past --
why had i been chosen?

                a time ago
              (now) effulgent
            host spat venom
        for (meager) infraction.

periodic attempts
     to exchange cordial nods
impassively ignored.

            invitation to partake
               pleasant testament

forgettable deed
        finally forgotten.

promptly ensconced
        near select cask,
    i awaited his arrival.

series of snaps
  shattered the darkening calm.
    soon discerned as
        concatenation of locks.

incandescent hajj
    had become
        irrevocable vendetta.

when i crumbled
 (as per schedule);
   ammonia ampoule
      delectably at the ready.

i must be sentient.

bowels of
  cretaceous caverns
    devoured
        orison of sterile shrieks.

              as
            candlelight
                succor
                    succumbed

        braille discernment
           disclosed like transgressors
              across
                  a diaspora of bones.

tell-tale torsion (r.f.)

True! --- nervous --- very, very dreadfully nervous I had been, and am ... ~ Edgar Allan Poe

terror,
raging;
unrelenting;
endless! ---

nerve
endings
remonstrate
venomous
obsequies,
usurping
sanity ---

venial
enmity
relentlessly
yelping,

voraciously
eviscerating
reason's
yolk

demonic
revenge;
execrable
agonies
deafen:
fleering,
ugsome,
lowering

lamentations
yowl

necrotic
entreaties
render
venal
obloquies;
unholy
susurrations,

infernal ...

hearken:
abhorrent
damnation

bestial
endeavor
echoes
(nevermore)

abysmal,
nefarious
doom

apprehends
me ...

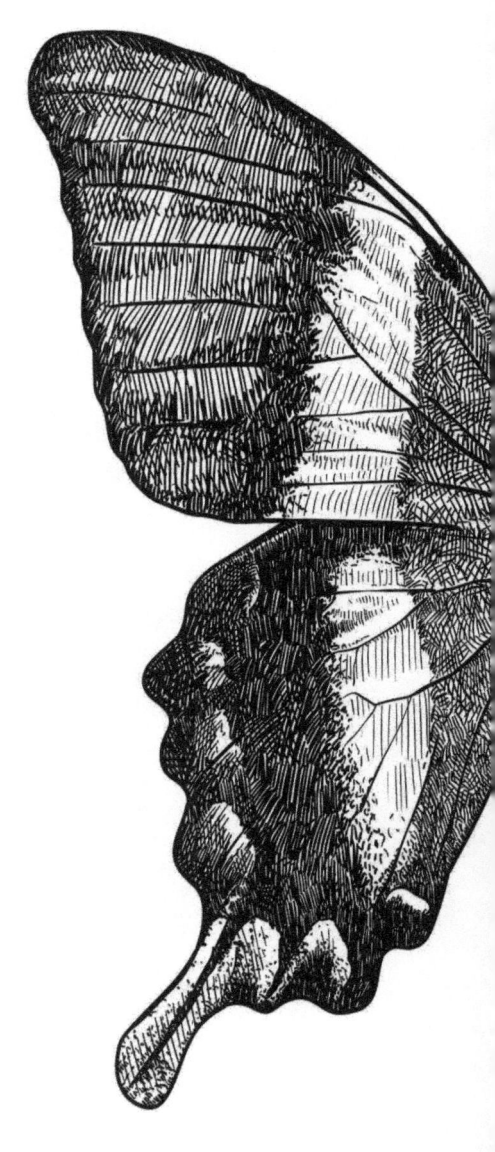

Sexton

identity crisis (c.s)

Saints have no moderation, nor do poets, just exuberance.

~ Anne Sexton

failing to be a word
                in his sonnet

catherine stood

                bereft

that she was nearly
                someone

devolution (r.f.)

It doesn't matter who my father was; it matters who I remember he was ~ Anne Sexton

halomonadaceae
      (a protobacteria newly discovered by nasa),
having mastered alchemic
integration of arsenic
into its dna,
thrives in mono lake, california
      (where arsenic levels average
              seventeen
                    parts per million)
under conditions in which
other forms of life
cannot survive.

google reports that
exobiologists the world over
are astounded.

arsenic
    (from the greek arsenikos,
        meaning 'masculine' and 'toxic')
is one of deadliest substances
known to man—
an untraceable, silent killer.

van gogh went crazy;
monet, blind;
emerald green
      (an arsenic-based pigment
          favored by Impressionists)

was to blame
    (merest exposure, it seems,
        causes irreparable harm).

both survived
    (albeit damaged),
creating works
of unassailable beauty
tinged with infinite pain.

i know what it is
to be awash in a sea of toxins;
to survive by integrating arsenic
into one's dna.

halomonadaceae
in mono lake, california?

those exobiologists
somehow missed:

i survived my father.

here, too
    (in the primordial lake of my
        emerald green memory),
lurks arsenikos dna
(unhallowed, alchemic
proof strands)—

homomonadaceae.

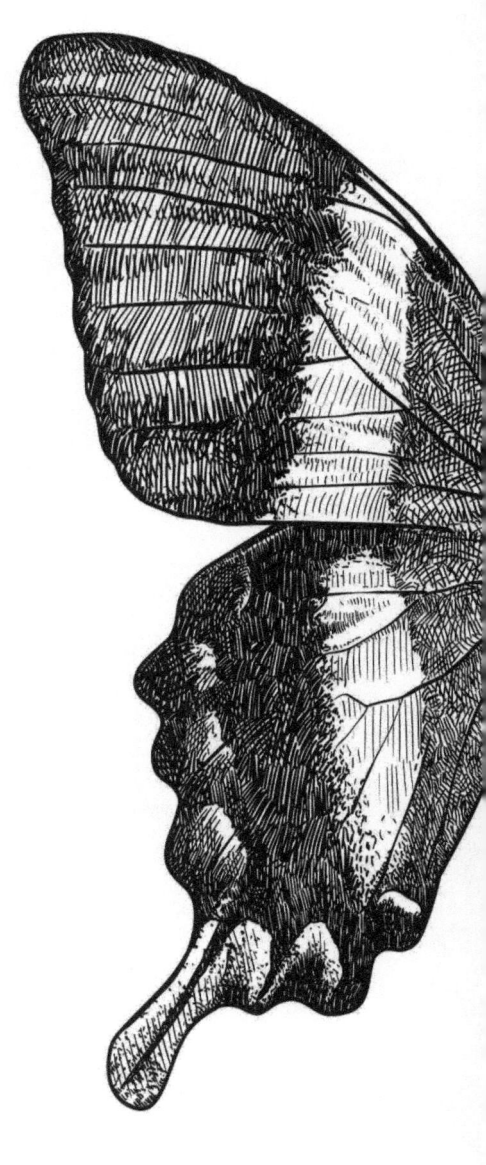

Neruda

incantation (c.s.)

I love you as certain dark things are to be loved, in secret, between the shadow and the soul

~ Pablo Neruda

   ... in the tangle

        of those serpentine hours

    when my eyes bled eruptions

when want seared the misbeliever

when stars illumed

        lost promises

when truth was blood, wheat and silver ...

i knew you would come

poieplegia (r.f.)

I love you in this way because I don't know any other way of loving. ~ Pablo Neruda

what i want
is to be luminous, sweeping;
to leave behind verses
translated from candlelit
palabros de amor.

what i fear
is that death, when it finds me,
will likely find me
still pulling shards of art from
the feet of
my puritan shame

(i have never
been able to write
from the waist down).

what i dream
is that
when i wake up tomorrow
the inside of my head
will be *sexy.*

what i seek
is macchu picchu;

what i find
is glastonbury.

what i hope
is that next time 'round
my pen will drip metric love juice
onto linen;

in this incarnation
i am lemon juice
on parchment,

needing heat and light
to bring out
my deeper
meaning.

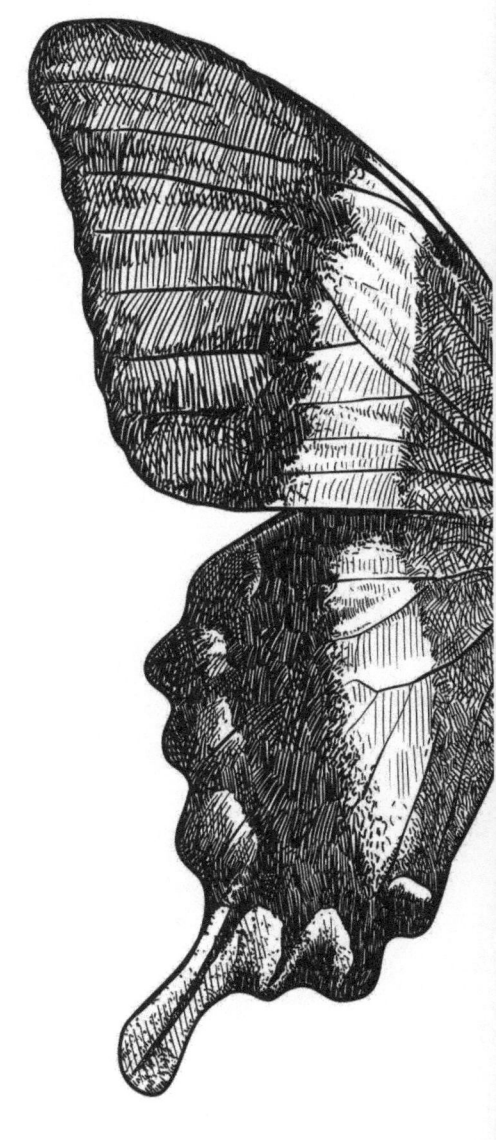

Shakespeare

tubular vision (r.f.)

Nothing either good or bad, but thinking makes it so
~ William Shakespeare

he was

a crazy man --

designed to feint and flail,

his outward self

(can a nylon cylinder *have* a self?)

a mirror image of

my inner bedlam

on the cell

with a friend

in the ell of a strip mall parking lot

picking up chinese take-out

with crazy man gyrating wildly

in the periphery,

i could not bring myself to

step out of the car

a vomitous, malignant rage was

darkening, swelling into

virulent parallax anguish

when, in the throes of

what could only have been

unprecedented celestial alignment,

crazy man tucked his head

under the eaves

and was briefly,

inexplicably

still ...

if he,

conceived for chaos,

could find even

the merest moment of

sanctified quietude,

how *dare* i persist

in psychic

entropy?

wailing wounded (c.s.)

These violent delights have violent ends . . .

~ William Shakespeare

i.

she came to me
a doe-eyed scar

an almond
sob

a page of scripture defiled by
glutinous
hands

she was
scant more than an armful,
mounted by shepherds, pit bulls
and mastiffs,
frothing.

obligatory screams had long been practiced.

each time
viscid tentacles
besieged
the shallow
wire crate,
her captor's
slithery chokehold
consecrated
another round
of clockwork rape

to satiate
lupine behemoths

,,, each time ...

she dissolved into
a colloquy of mania

the consummation of horror was well-rehearsed:
a murder of penetrations, exquisitely familiar

ii.

a life spent
knowing the certainty of human cruelty
meant 'rescue' was just a mottled form
of repetition
and 'better'
non-existent

when
the untended cage door
miraculously opened
she sought
alien grass
and found a whiff of kindness

but rather than
mouthing the beatitudes
common to all God's creatures

(we, the species,
gave her no reason

to accept anything with gratitude;
rather, with nightmares always looming),

she shrieked from a bottomless soul
weeping in the shadows
of kindred crushed
she threw herself over and over
at my apartment door.

iii.

knowing, like she,
the certainty of human cruelty,
i sat, unmovable—
wordless—but making
whispered sounds
only heard by
desperate detritus

realizing that we were fluent in
agony's vocabulary—
the certainty of mutual anguish—
created a space to tender
disfigured breath
and scabrous tears—

opening the door
            for
                      an inviolate embrace.

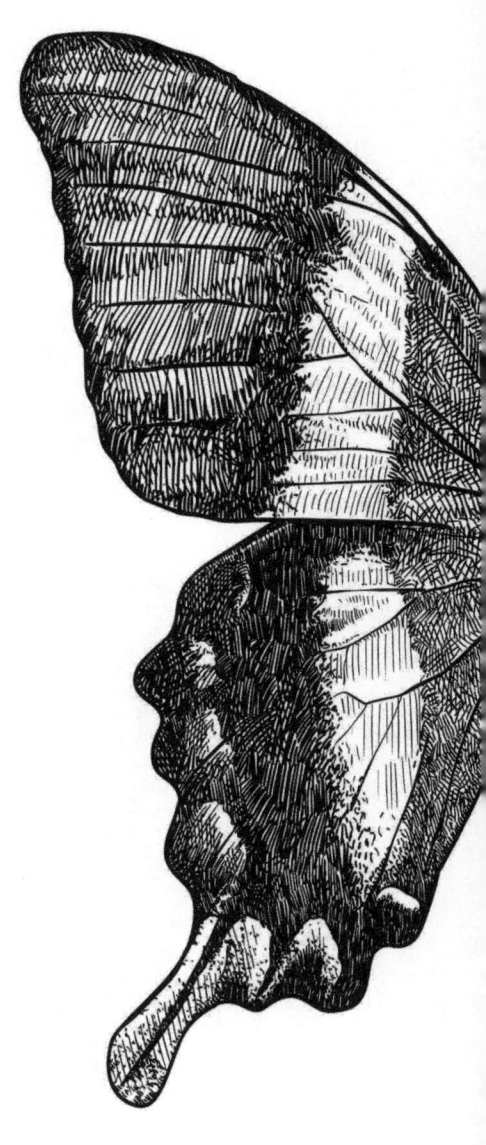

Twain

basilisk (r.f.)

*The elastic heart of youth cannot be compressed
into one constrained shape long at a time.*
~ Mark Twain

après-midi,
nu,
en biarritz ,,.

about to take a mindless selfie of
my toes on vacation
avec la mer on the horizon,
i was dissuaded
by what lay outside the frame:

languid body, pale and amorphous;
rheumatoid knees; flaccid peg
(long disused, but full of memory);
pasty ankles, undefined;
talon-nailed toes, crooked—

sending a selfie into
pixelated ether
is risky business!

can the CIA conjure up peripheral ghosts?
do puerile, moon-faced techies
chuckle and snort
in clandestine low-light labs?

and what of photoshop?
just the thought of my lower extremities
reimaged by a skilled manipulator ...

mon dieu!

having narrowly averted
a glaring lapse in better judgment,
i resumed basking and dreamt of
walking on water ...

coronation (c.s.)

All kings is mostly rapscallions.

~ Mark Twain

what to do with
        a broken diadem?

wallow
in the
     gone?

lament
majestic
     particles?

beg
ineluctable
     sun?

exalt
the weary gatherer
   with equal need
        to heal.

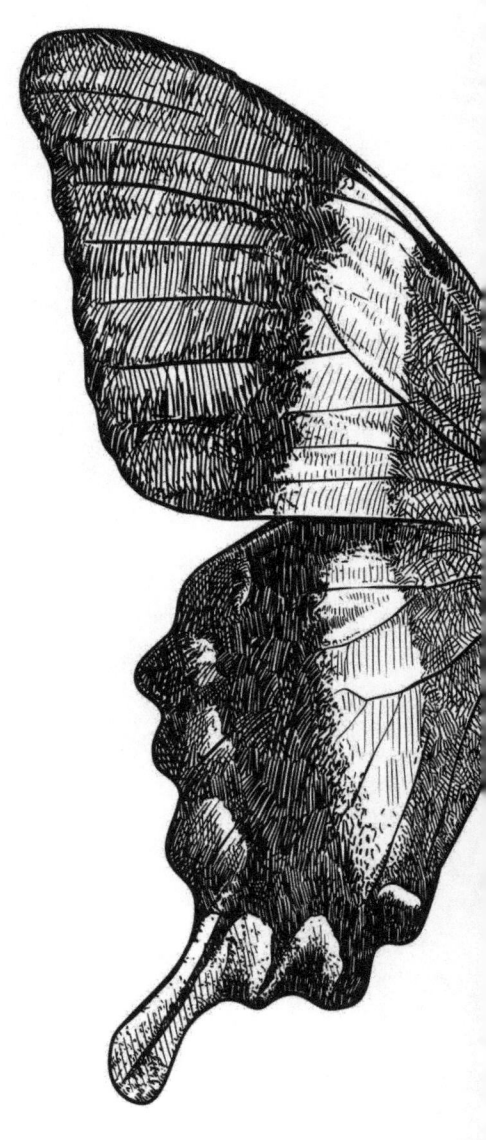

Carroll

gehenna (r.f.)

"In my youth," Father William replied to his son, "I feared it might injure the brain; But now that I'm perfectly sure I have none, Why, I do it again and again." ~ Lewis Carroll

these days
he is alternately
bewildered
and amiable,
his rage
waxing
and waning
in spasmodic parody
of the succubi
he once hosted.

i, too, am only
dimly aware:

is it because
i find myself
more amnesic
each year
that i so revile
his burgeoning
dementia?

karmic justice would dictate
that he be fully present
for this, the deserved loneliness
of his golden years;
conversely,
the drifting, driveling relic he has become
posthumously sates a lost boy's lust
for retribution …

the horror lies in knowing—
either way—
it is i who cannot let him go.

radical acceptance (c.s.)

Begin at the beginning and go on till you come to the end; then stop. ~ Lewis Carroll

hood, hawk

        sparrow

                sparrow ≥≥>

((sparrow))

                    ... sparrow ...

      sparrow

            sp   a   rrow

                  hawk, hood

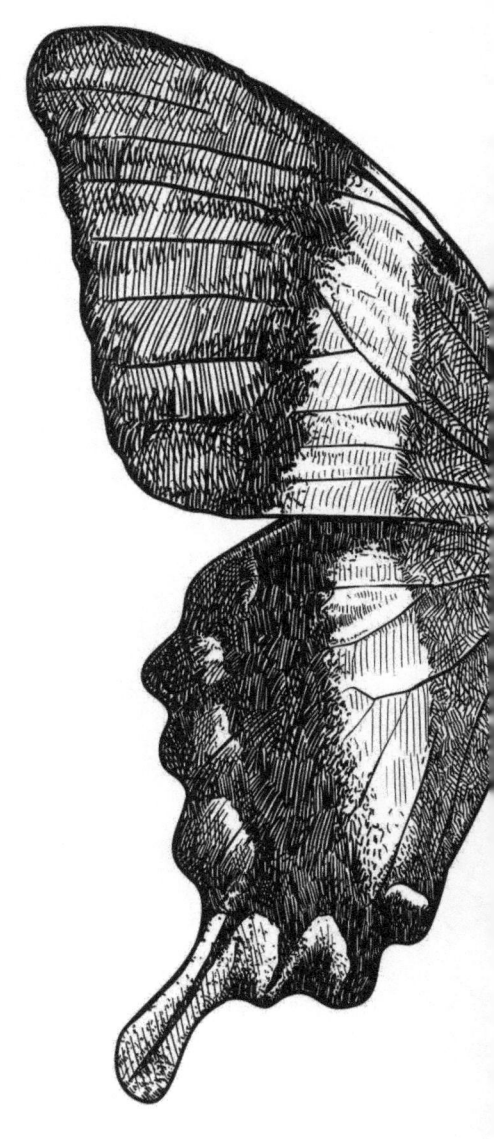

Thomas

welsh-flecked romance (c.s.)

With the dew, come back, the cock on his shoulder, it was all shining, it was Adam and maiden. ~ Dylan Thomas

in the laughing house
strewn among
  the plum-dappled
peach trickling meadow,
a thicket of blackberried
hummingbirds
          steal my form

     that i may gaze
     at glimmers of hyacinth hair
     and the ripple of farm hued
     body, sawing and bailing, in
     briny brilliantine hallow

till ash evening
falls
and i return to the
   dragonfly blight of
onyx ribboned hills
   that fill me with the
         quarry of your absence ~

tracing unkissed lips, pale
in the time-skewered dusk.

polypodieœ (r.f.)

Time held me green and dying
Though I sang in my chains like the sea.
~ Dylan Thomas

i did not think to stay, close in that sylvan frond circle;
did not think to cede one soft, lingering sun-dappled
    sigh
to imprint upon my vernal sight
the glory of that glen
shimmering in late august dimmet
before dark vagaries of time diminished unto dusk
its elfin enchantment and fawn-sweet sheltering
    incense,
lost in the sweep of progress,
fiddleheads grown tuneless and sere.

when i, yet green in the ways of a world beyond the
    wood,
first beheld that faerie ring in chary brindled splendor,
my young heart brimmed with ebullient song,
dancing the circle round
in luxuriant blithe abandon,
the fey, feathered plumes caressing pale twig legs
    even as
my burgeoning bliss heralded plenary innocence
to canopied branches and
chiming birds giddy with morning dew.

wounding years hence i remember, they were sacred,
    those ferns
light terpsichore, pale fronds waving gaily, sunlit
    nymphs
all dancing, gamboling in the breeze
and whispering rare lays.
and often since i was callow there
where down fiddleheads caressed my shell-pink ears
    with rondels,
still in fair dreams i hear, mystic beyond fable, those
    rustling
troubadours so sweet, oh so merry
knelling heaven and joy.

and when i awake, and i quell, all my sun-dappled
    ferns
are long gone, are passed, the gems of lost boyhood:
    they are swift
fading, as if never they feathered
that bright clearing of dreams.
then at once comes back such dashing hope
thence to dust again fleeting as motes in the waning
    stream
of the sun, as it fades, its dying tendrils laid to waste
all in the withering brown spinney
once swathed in green and light.

though seldom am i carefree or blameless in this
    mean world
borne of an ardent thirst for lucre and the lure of fame,
when alone and pining for solace
i conjure shaded vales
from air and mind and the scourge of time
and though i am blown, i may yet return, to circled
    fronds
with all their lissome waving in dew and rich golden
    dawn
before the sodden sway of waste mouldered
purity in its bloom.

what need i fear, in the crush of toil, as long as fronds
    dance
gaily in a circle made new by green innocence
    recalled
on a day that is ever shining
that awake or asleep
comes forgiving and free as a sweet balm
to bid sluggish legs remember paths through the
    brimming wood
and as I was once a stripling in that sea of singing
    ferns
still am i wreathed in bowers
as i rush to my close with delight.

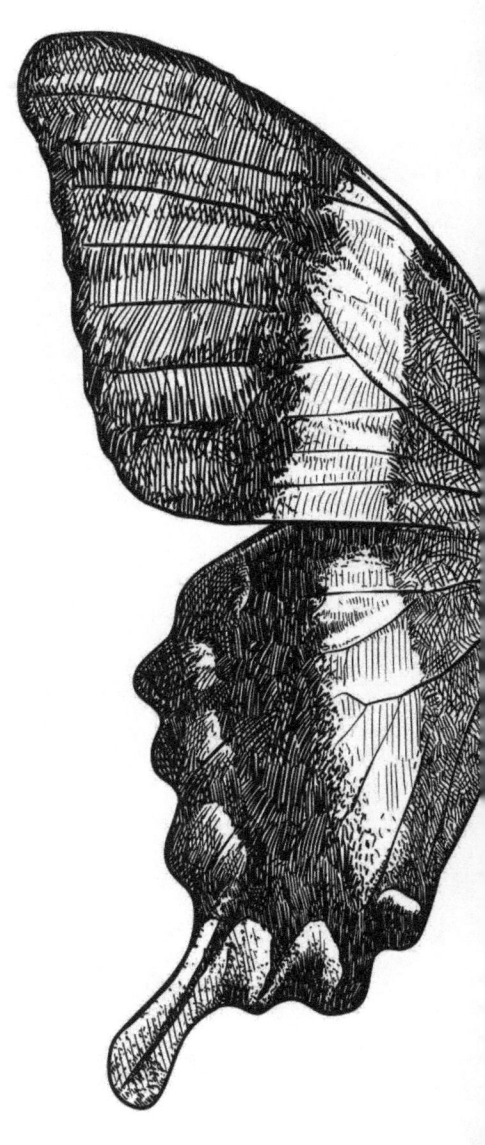

Miller

hyde (r.f.)

I have given you my soul: leave me my name!
~ Arthur Miller

for half the world to live in light,
the other half must dwell in darkness

so it goes:

your felicity and my rage
are conjoined

your enchantment—your glow—
never reaches me
yet i claw at any reflected glimmer,
any scintilla of *you*
as if it were the essence of all life

i tell myself
i have made my peace with shadow;
my place and my purpose are clear,
and yet ...

i cannot call you brother;
I cannot call you kin
(you are simply 'other'—
me without, you within) ...

turn your face toward a sunbeam, jekyll;
drink your precious light
but do not suppose i languish here,
crepuscular and effete:
i am learning to dance in darkness
for every dawn
is armageddon
postponed ...

cart blench (c.s.)

What a woman! They broke the mold when they made her.
~ Arthur Miller

grip-inseminated
       shopping cart
             snorts at the starting gate:
                 wilted iceberg warnings
                         frenetically dismissed

succulent imaginings of booty beckon—

  (two-for-one
       lunchmeat
             extravaganza;
                 belly-dented can bin plunge;
                 deftly strategized
                       tuesday super-specials)

ii

careening
      over the finish line;
            mistress of 'all the trimmings'
                  cannot comprehend
the blithe unveiling
                         of defeat:

        aisles plumbed by granddame legions

        shelves teeming cyclonic refuse

  (house-keeping reverie
silently dissevered ...)

iii

    at
           cusp of
                  cashier confrontation

traces of
        moribund coupons
                strew path
                      to
                              full-price
                                      surrender.

Thoreau

a very thoreau haiku (r.f.)

I went to the woods because I wished to live,

deliberately to front only the essential facts of life,

and see if I could not learn what it had to teach, and not,

when I came to die, discover that I had not lived.

~ Henry David Thoreau

two years on, one truth:

limnologist's irony -

nature watches *us.*

cultural exchange (c.s.)

It is only when we forget all our learning that we begin to know. ~ Henry David Thoreau

i.

no ammunition

M-1 useless

scant yards away

adolescent

leaps from trench

hell bent to ram seven inches of steel

(into

not a person

but a thing)

screaming *Gai-jin!*

ii.

20 below

sopped in sweat

circlets of white

frame inert pupils

-- lips akimbo

-- torn paper skin

-- air depleted

silently screaming

not to be seen

in enemy terrain –

one glimmer away

from slaughter

iii.

the kill

should have been textbook:

instead,

bayonets blazed and

two faces

frozen in morbid astonishment

crumbled in tandem

to corpses

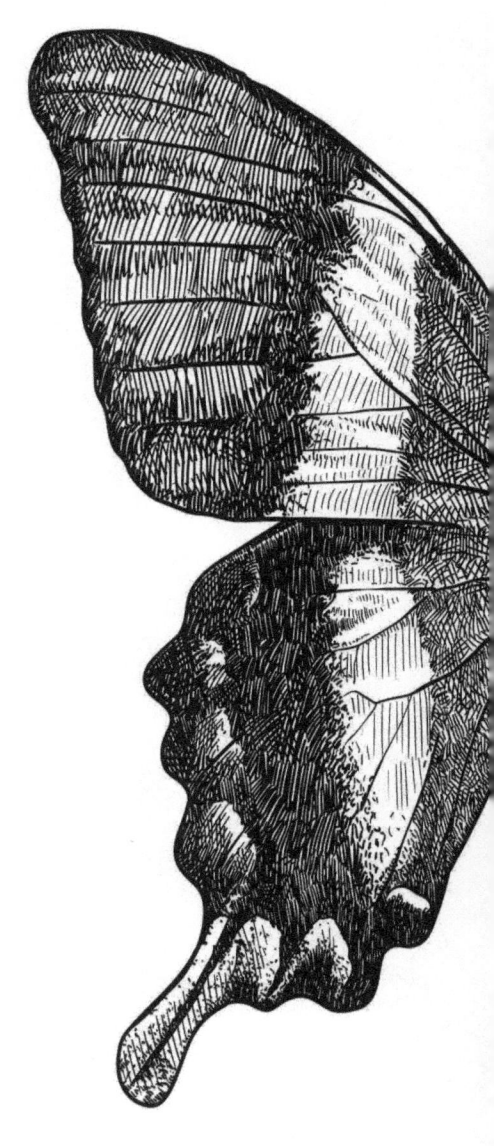

Brooks

evangeline (r.f.)

You were born, you had body, you died.
It is just that you never giggled or planned or cried.

~ Gwendolyn Brooks

for thirty-five days
we held her,

knowing she could not stay—

drinking the pearled nectar
of her seeming perfection
deeply, reverently;

murmuring euphoric orisons
even as she lay dying
in our embrace.

only a stem
where her brain should have been;

we heard the diagnosis
but somehow

vain hope drove our prayers,
fitting them
with waxen wings.

her life
was a bated breath;

her ascension
a whispered grace -

exhaling,
we wept more
in awe
than with grieving.

ephemeral seraph,
fallen to earth—

for thirty-five days
we held her,

knowing she could not stay.

the tragedy of the raft of the medusa (c.s.)

Believe that even in my deliberateness, I was not deliberate
~ Gwendolyn Brooks

rags of madness

    flail at barren clouds

   shuttered

      in

    vermillion

a father dons

   a rotting son

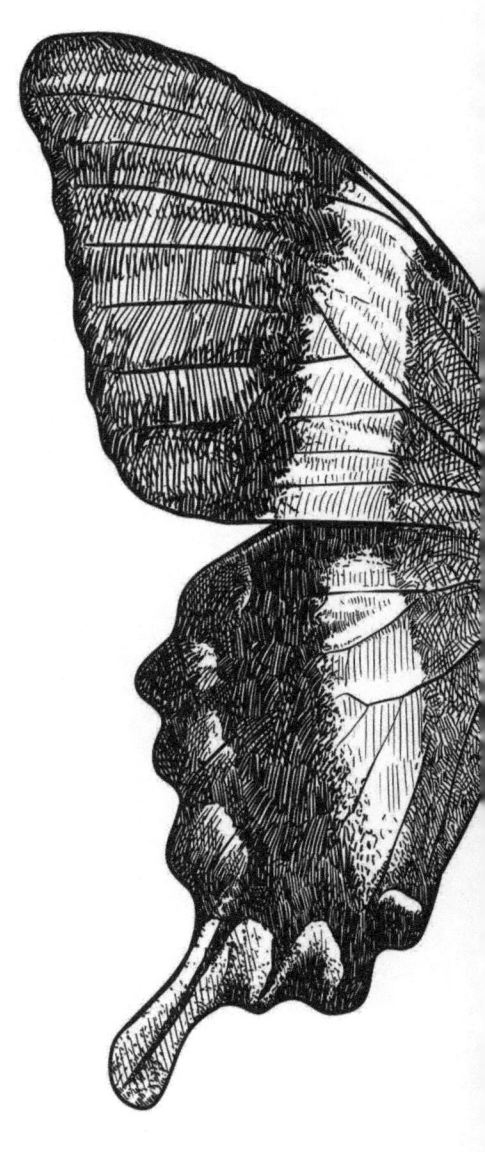

Orwell

escher's oubliette (r.f.)

That thing in Room 101 is the worst thing in the world.
~ George Orwell

the room
in itself
is not
frightening;

it is
the *emptiness*
that terrifies.

these walls
guard their secrets
as whores
enshroud
remembered
innocents:

wan ectoplasmic wisps,
their mute malisons
paralyzing.

in the silence,
i sometimes imagine that
this room
(this womb of fear)
emits
unhallowed susurrations—

that wraiths compete for
the succoring sweat
of blind panic,
feasting on weeping
saprophytic pustules
of my rheumic despair.

the room
in itself
is not
frightening;

it is only
this pullulating
sense:

as
i am
in the room,

the room is
in me ...

impolitic (c.s.)

*Doublethink means the power of holding
two contradictory beliefs in one's mind simultaneously
and accepting both of them.
~ George Orwell*

in mustard capris

    a faux brunette

takes time to place the salon copy

of People magazine

    on a stainless steel shelf next to the steaming basin

to inquire where the crouched form at her feet

was from:

      "Saigon."

she smiles and resumes her study of

      the Sexiest Man in America,

    oblivious to the dark child

        running a razor

          under her heel

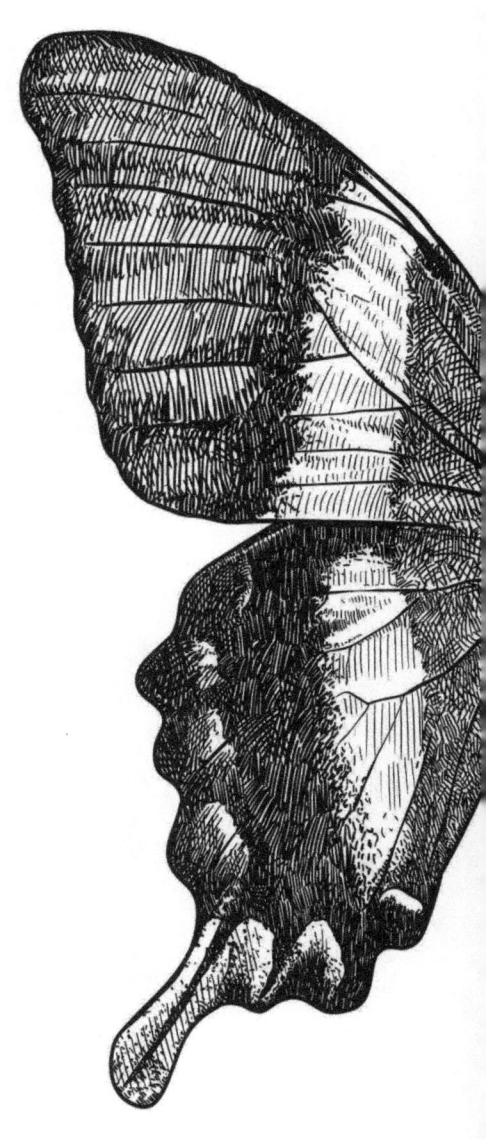

Lee

coquette (c.s.)

I think I'll be a clown when I get grown
~ Harper Lee

45
 years old
Crown Heights, born
      an' bred
brand new perky
        plump boobies
botox macerated smile

never been to Paris
    or Marseilles
      or Provence --

 content in knowing
     she never left

flamé chignon
crème beret, just so;
'eiffel lush' lipstick
mint frou frou blouson

               adorned *dans la mode*
            she embarks in *chansons*

taxis, always taxis --
for a dime
they'll believe
any crap accent
stifling smirk
at the freak show
saucily sauntering 'bye!'

Jules and Jim
        at 19
and that's all it took
La Binoche of Brooklyn
pour toujours
            am i.

exogenesis (r.f.)

You can choose your friends but you sho' can't choose your family, an' they're still kin to you no matter whether you acknowledge 'em or not, and it makes you look right silly.

~ Harper Lee

at bay beneath the floribunda

in the seventh summer of my wounding

an unexpected snakeskin

propped in the dead gray notch

of some previous year's pruning

sucked even the memory of breath

from my sapling frame

too frightened to flee,

frozen in the shade of

its sinister perfection,

i raised one trembling finger

watching in disbelief

as it crumbled to dust

at my touch

today,

still poisoned by

remembered venom,

how do i touch

this hollow brown shell

that was my father?

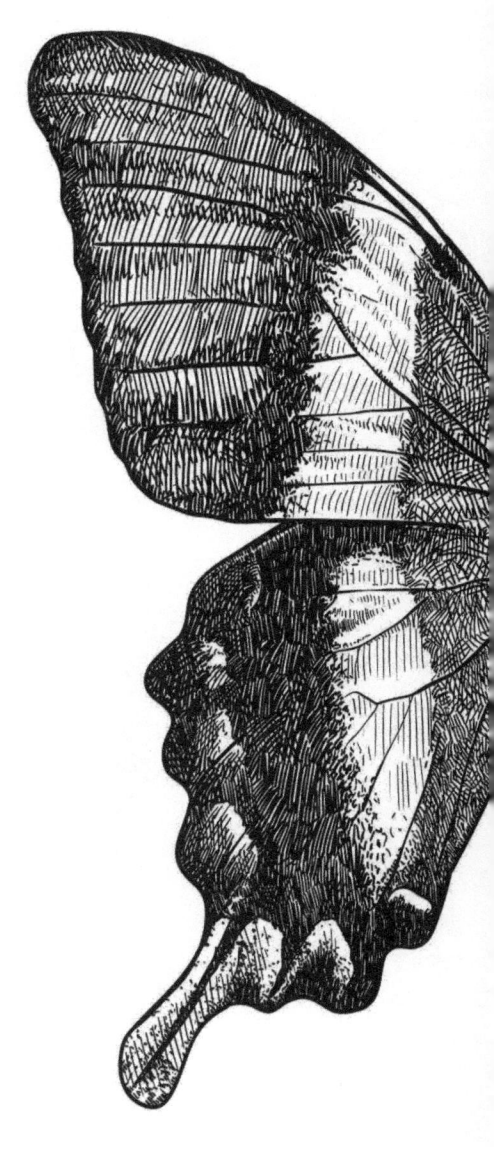

Brontë

scream (c.s.)

Terror made me cruel . . . ~ Emily Brontë

i.

                breath
pause
      breath
            pause
                  breath
          breath
pause
                brea ...

i was eight years old

walking down Tremont Avenue.

a car had swerved
and there, at what seemed

the epicenter of the world --
        two halves of a dog.

there are two kinds of screams:

one fights death.

one begs it.

possessed,

i seized a trash can lid

        and remained
          inert,

            fruitlessly
               beseeching God

                      to finish

                    what i could not.

               ii.

        breath
pause
          breath
               pause
    breath
        pau ...

it was a mother --

a childless mother
cradling her just-dead child.

the car had sped
over malefic
      iced streets –
           saying nothing

        crushing everything.

babe shielded
    from morgue reapers;
 mandates
   for reliquary flesh denied;

night skies swelled
    with tumid
      derangements.

 daily imprecations
    hissed at traitorous Savior.

in time,
   rage consumed grief.

        iii.

   the dog died;

    the mother abandoned being.

two godforsaken
    strangers

bound by
   the limitless horrors
      of mortality--

 one strewn,

    one screaming.

what singing really is (r.f.)

It was not the thorn bending to the honeysuckles, but the honeysuckles embracing the thorn.

~ Emily Brontë

ten years old
in my grandmother's kitchen
on a sunday afternoon:
she was hymn-singing
over her prototype waring mixer:
"rock of aaaaaaaaaaaaaaaaaaaaaaages … "

her voice was not unlike
glass marbles rolling down
concrete steps.

at the precise apex of her raucous devotion,
she paused to take a breath,
allowing the mixer to rest
for the merest of moments—
just long enough for me,
in childish treble,
to utter one brutal question:
"grandmother, why do you always sing
when you know everyone wants you to *stop*?"
silence followed;

i watched her deflate slightly,

shoulders sagging under faded housedress;

then, she set down the mixer

as if it were a wounded bird and,

after an eternal moment,

turned, embraced me

(folding me to her gingham-clad bosom

until I was faint from oxygen deprivation),

pinched my childish apple cheek

ever-so-gently

with the hermetic precision

only grandmothers can muster,

looked deep into my beer-bottle-brown eyes

(so like my mother's),

and said:

"lambie ... *lambie ...*

when the good lord said

make a joyful noise,

he didn't specify a key ... "

that day,

i understood

for the first time

what singing really *is ...*

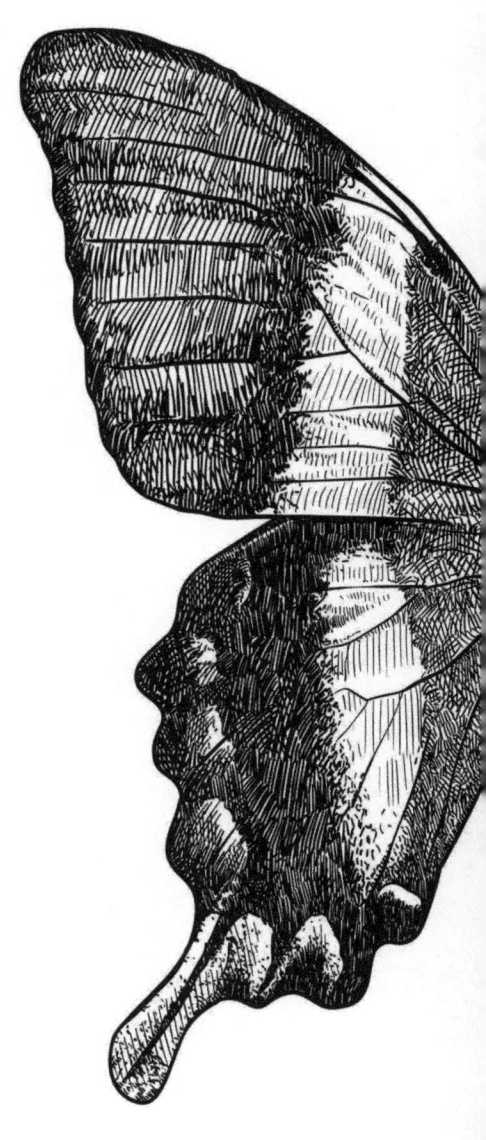

Dickens

fezziwig regards his missus (r.f.)

In came Mrs. Fezziwig, one vast substantial smile.
~ Charles Dickens

she is golden to my eye;

coruscant autumn's

corrugated grace

etching the corners

of her summered smile;

these days,

these sage-smoked days of

amber, russet and

burnished auburn,

she is dearer to me

than ever she was

in halcyon spring.

in the slant apricot rays

of our enduring devotion,

an abundant harvest

of remembered joys

shimmers and gleams:

love's promise, kept.

she is golden to my eye;

aureate; her lustre augmenting

the piquant sweetness

of august longing.

these days,

these waning,

wintered days of

wanton wishes and whys –

she is surety,

substance and

solace.

she is golden to my eye;

newly minted in each

sunset reverie –

at *carpe diem's* close,

she is,

was,

always will be

the diadem

of my seasoned joys.

urchin (c.s.)

I have been bent and broken, but - I hope - into a better shape. ~ Charles Dickens

christened as scum,
    six-year-old quintessence of filth
      sensed ineffable
        natural selection
          as pathetic pauper
              paused—

    uncharted attempts
      to conjure a whiff of dignity
        met raucous derision
          from fellow East End denizens
            as 'civilized' guards
              (barring respectable entry)
                smugly scoffed …

    without allies
      to mount counterattack,
        deflated escapee
          succumbed
            to colloquy of take

          but

            the unassailable lust

      to be *seen*

would not abate:

with each assault from waste-swelled vessel,
with each taunt to tempt blood-sopped combat,
with each demand for rag-strewn blanket—

'no'

ascended.

Steinbeck

parable (c.s.)

[T]he dust came in so thinly that it could not be seen in the air, and it settled like pollen ... ~ John Steinbeck

i.

release from the kitchen table imminent,

      strategy fixed for
        a bee-line dash
          to the irascible
            rust-drenched
              swing set,

    i whacked my Fred Flintstone glass
    on a misjudged aluminum corner,
        surrendering translucent slivers
            to (just-unfurled)
              pistachio linoleum

as my mother clucked over each heart-staked shard
    (simultaneously scouring every inch of
      her coveted tiles for damage),
          i soundlessly witnessed
  my animated buddy
    being dumped into
           a stainless steel graveyard

knowing any plea
    for a pause
      would be unheeded,
    i hid behind
        our (just-bought) back porch rocker—
            a deluge of virgin sobs.

ii.

   the drive
     offered neither comfort
      nor threat

  i rang the doorbell
    and asked to meander –
  the back porch teemed
    with dust-swollen things

drawn to a wobbly column
   of long-unopened
     children's books,
 i sank into the weary rocking chair,
    seeking reacquaintance

   despite crackling pages,
    the wisdom of the Learning Tree
     still rang true:

    Cindy-Lou Who
      remained
   the apogee of
innocence.

cantankerous
rabbit

  snared yet again by
    implacable tar baby.

i saw Brer's fate differently—

    the legacy of
        a child's barren weeping

            for a shattered companion
    a child nurtured in
        immured dismissals and innate
denial—
                              was
        a life of casualty.

        iii.

    the anecdote
  (reconfigured for Christmas party banter)
  had become pithy justification for
    a cacophony of adult indiscretions.

'my glass –my pain--my entitlement'
    morphed into drifting particles of
        self-assault.

        iv.

books restored to skewed anonymity,
    i walked past the dangling swing,
        glanced at the militantly defended floor,

found our never-lost moment,
    and began to relinquish scars.

congruence (r.f.)

As happens sometimes, a moment settled and hovered and remained for much more than a moment. ~John Steinbeck

i suppose, to an onlooker,
the scene might have seemed odd:
two brothers, lying side by side
on a weary shag carpet,
gazing up through a heat-hazed skylight
at stars they felt had
(until that night)
forsaken them utterly.

we were holding hands—
something we had never done before—
just *lying* there, holding hands, gazing up and
tossing occasional syllables
across the sheltering blackness
until, gradually, the vastness between us
became something less than infinite.

it might have been an hour,
it might have been ten;
what was most important
about that moment
was this:
for the first time,
thirty-two years into our shared-DNA journey,
under those unassailable skylight stars,
we connected across the void—
dissolving our binary brokenness into
vitruvian fraternal synchrony.
syllables evolved into sentences,

confessions and revelations followed,
absolution twinkled, and—
in one fleeting, filial scintilla of forever—
our twinned universes of pain
coalesced, chiming the celestial harmonics
possible only when cain and abel forgive.

it ended
as benignly as it began:
bladder pressing,
bathroom down the hall,
mood broken,
stars dimmed.

he was dead by his own hand
one month later:
it turns out
one of those stars
was a meteor.

two decades hence,
i still search for clues
in the smoking crater,
obsessing as i sift through ash:
if that brother-loves-brother moment
really was as i have written it here,
wouldn't i have *seen*?

wouldn't i have *known*?

questions—
stars—

eternal.

Swenson

purgatorio (c.s.)

We play in the den of the Gods and snort at death.
~ May Swenson

   my Lady of blinding optimism

   have mercy on me

   for i now seek

    a glimpse of that which makes clockwork dawn
                                 this morning

       blush in the awe that graces endings.

   i try to see sashay of
                last leaves
      as mottled canopy
   of hope,

   to perceive night sky aglow

   with billions of
         hallow glimmerings

   but peering
   skyward
    i see
         dying leaves as inchoate particles

               and
                      heaven pockmarked.

    i look for gasp,
i find
  disease.

      i am so weary.

    stripes of
      apostasy

 sear fresh

incredulity of
   grandeur in
       abasement—
mock
     plangent vows to sacred ephemera—

 pity
     vainglorious penitent
        immured in unnumbered doubts.

all that makes

moment of

flesh renunciation

epiphany or curse.

gautam (r.f.)

Body my house
my horse my hound
what will I do
when you are fallen

~ May Swenson

we waited

without breath, hyper-focused,

cataloguing each rise and fall

of his butterfly-wing chest

as if it were his last—

as if our communal psychic freeze-frame

might somehow hold him here a moment longer

we checked, rechecked our pained faces,

transmuting our dread into

tight-lipped masks of feigned acceptance,

smoothing creases in our clothes

as if death might be kinder should it find

us, his attendants,

fresh and open

when

at last

the moment came,

it was what none of us could have foreseen:

he did not grimace, twitch,

or strain against unfulfilled promises;

he simply turned his head toward us and smiled,

giving off a light

we could only interpret as more life—greater life—

and we realized, with a collective sigh,

the hypocrisy inherent

in mourning death.

Sources

Poe:
The Cask of Amontillado (c.s.)
The Tell-tale Heart (r.f.)

Sexton:
The Saints Come Marching In (c.s.)
Journal entry, 1972 (r.f.)

Neruda:
Ten Love Poems (c.s.)
One Hundred Love Sonnets: XVII (r.f.)

Shakespeare:
Hamlet, Act II, scene ii (r.f.)
Romeo and Juliet (c.s.)

Twain:
The Adventures of Tom Sawyer (r.f.)
The Adventures of Huckleberry Finn (c.s.)

Carroll:
You are Old, Father William (r.f.)
Alice's Adventures in Wonderland (c.s.)

Thomas:
Fern Hill (c.s., r.f.)

Miller:
The Crucible (r.f.)
Death of A Salesman (c.s.)

Thoreau:
Walden; or Life in the Woods (r.f.)
Journal: 4 October, 1859 (c.s.)

Brooks:
The Mother (r.f., c.s.)

Orwell:
1984 (r.f., c.s.)

Lee:
To Kill a Mockingbird (c.s., r.f.)

Brontë:
Wuthering Heights (c.s., r.f.)

Dickens:
A Christmas Carol (r.f.)
Great Expectations (c.s.)

Steinbeck:
The Grapes of Wrath (c.s.)
Of Mice and Men (r.f.)

Swenson:
To Confirm a Thing (c.s.)
Question (r.f.)

Acknowledgments

The following poems by Constance Stadler have been previously published:

Coquette (Shadow Archer Press, 2009)

welsh-flecked romance (Tinted Steam 2009)

The following poems by Rich Follett have been previously published:

devolution (Poetic Diversity, November 2019)

Evangeline (Sugar Mule # 47)

Poieplegia (Edgar Allan Poet #2, Red Fez # 59)

tubular vision (2nd Los Angeles Poetry Beach Festival Anthology, NoVa Bards Anthology 2022)

About the Authors

Rich Follett is a Middle School Theatre Arts teacher who has written poems and songs for more than fifty years. He was born on Long Island and moved after college to Virginia, where he serves as the official Poet Laureate for his adopted hometown of Strasburg. His poems have been featured in numerous online and print journals, including BlazeVox, the Montucky Review, the Willows Wept Review (Pushcart nominee), and the late Felino Soriano's CounterExample Poetics, for which he was a featured artist. Rich co-authored *Responsorials* with Constance Stadler (2009) and two solo collections, *Silence, Inhabited* (2011), and *Human &c.* (2013) through NeoPoiesis Press, and *Photo-Ku* (2016) through NightWing Publications.

He is featured in the ODU Virginia Poets Database at https://digitalcommons.odu.edu/virginiapoets. Information and publications at www.richfollett.com

Constance Stadler is the author and co-author of eight books of poetry in print and online format, including Descending Upward (NightWing Publications) and Responsorials (with Rich Follett, NeoPoiesis Press). She was awarded honors in the 2023 International Erbacce Prize competition, which numbered over 14,000 submissions. Constance holds a doctorate in International Studies from New York University and lives in the beautiful Shenandoah Valley.

Her relationship with poetry dates back to early teenage years, when she was given a copy of *The Collected Works of Dylan Thomas*, which still sits, dog-eared, on her bookshelf.

www.ingramcontent.com/pod-product-compliance
Lightning Source LLC
LaVergne TN
LVHW041340080426
835512LV00006B/546